KU-389-470

Indoor Cats

Christine Church

Distributed in the UNITED STATES to the Pet Trade by T.F.H. Publications, Inc., 1 TFH Plaza, Neptune City, NJ 07753; on the Internet at www.tfh.com; in CANADA by Rolf C. Hagen Inc., 3225 Sartelon St., Montreal, Quebec H4R 1E8; Pet Trade by H & L Pet Supplies Inc., 27 Kingston Crescent, Kitchener, Ontario N2B 2T6; in ENGLAND by T.F.H. Publications, PO Box 74, Havant PO9 5TT; in AUSTRALIA AND THE SOUTH PACIFIC by T.F.H. (Australia), Pty. Ltd., Box 149, Brookvale 2100 N.S.W., Australia; in NEW ZEALAND by Brooklands Aquarium Ltd., 5 McGiven Drive, New Plymouth, RD1 New Zealand; in SOUTH AFRICA by Rolf C. Hagen S.A. (PTY.) LTD., P.O. Box 201199, Durban North 4016, South Africa; in JAPAN by T.F.H. Publications. Published by T.F.H. Publications, Inc.

MANUFACTURED IN THE
UNITED STATES OF AMERICA
BY T.F.H. PUBLICATIONS, INC.

Contents

Photographers: Glen Axelrod, Joan Balzarini, Christine Church, Jacquie DeLillo, Isabelle Francais, Gillian Lisle, Robert Pearcy, Vince Serbin, Aimee Strickland, Linda Sturdy, John Tyson

Introduction: Why Indoors?

There are more than 60 million cat owners in the US today, and more than half of them keep their cats strictly indoors. At one time, only a select few cat owners allowed their cats no access to the outdoors. The belief was that cats possess a wild nature, and to lock them behind closed doors is the equivalent of imprisonment. Cats worked as mousers for the most part, had litter after litter of kittens in barns, and drank milk straight from the cow.

But as human lifestyles changed and cities became more populated, with people living in apartments and high-rises where outdoor access was not as convenient a commodity, cat ownership grew and changed. Cats increased in popularity as pets because of their value as companions coupled with their ease of care. Cats did not need to be walked or obedience-trained, and they did not make noise or take up a lot of room. And most

At one time, cats typically worked as mousers, living in barns and having litter after litter of kittens.

Cats exposed to the outdoors are more at risk of contracting diseases such as feline leukemia virus or rabies.

Today, the outdoors is full of hazards to cats, from deadly cars to predatory coyotes.

As lifestyles changed, cat ownership changed. People realized that their cats did not have to go out to be happy.

importantly, cats could stay indoors, never having to step outside. Increasingly, people realized that their cats did not have to go out to be happy.

Also, as populations grew and traffic increased, dangers to cats became more prevalent. Cats were being hit by cars in larger numbers, and they were also trapped under the hoods of cars. City cats are now in the greatest danger, but even country cats aren't always safe. Though some cats still live in barns, country cat lovers, too, are starting to see the benefits to keeping their precious pets indoors. A wild animal, such as a coyote or an eagle, doesn't know the difference between your cat and a wild rabbit. A meal is a meal. Traps set for raccoons and other wild animals also do not discriminate as to what type of animal they ensnare.

Pesticides sprayed on plants can be very dangerous to an unsuspecting kitty. Hunters have accidentally shot pets they mistook for wild animals. The danger list is as endless for country cats as it is for city cats, who also have to deal with more hazards than just cars.

All cats, whether they live in the city or the country, can become plagued by parasites such as fleas and mites. Keeping cats indoors decreases this risk (though it may not completely eliminate it, especially if you have a dog or other animals—or even children—that are coming in and out of the house on a regular basis). Cats exposed to the outdoors and to other cats are more at risk of contracting diseases such as feline leukemia virus, a disease that is spread through saliva contact and is one of the biggest cat killers in this country. Rabies is a great concern in most of the country, and many states are just now beginning to recognize and do something about this, making rabies vaccines a legal requirement.

So, because of these and many more dangers not listed here, it is no wonder that keeping cats indoors has become such a popular notion. Indoor cats have more than twice the average life expectancy of an outdoor cat (5 to 8 years for an outdoor cat, 15 to 18 for an indoor cat) and are happier and healthier. However, they require different care than the outdoor cat. They need more love and attention, and thus they make better companions. Watch an indoor cat lazing in a windowsill or sitting on top of the television with that perfectly content look on her face, and you won't doubt the benefits of keeping your cat indoors—for you as well as your cat.

Just watch an indoor cat lazing in a windowsill with that perfectly content look on her face, and you won't doubt the benefits of keeping your cat indoors.

Behavior and Training

Nothing is perfect, and with the advent of the indoor cat came certain dilemmas not before known to owners of outdoor cats. Every new idea has its bugs to be worked out, and once cats began to be kept as indoor pets, owners discovered that they had certain behavioral differences from their outdoor counterparts.

The highest incidence of behavioral problems occurs in cats that have been outdoors most of their lives and are then converted to indoor-only cats. Unlike with people, it's rather difficult to explain to a cat why her environment has so dramatically changed. Households that are overcrowded, whether with too many cats, people, or other animals can also produce stressful reactions in the cats who reside there. But even cats that have always been indoors can develop behavioral problems, just as outdoor cats can and do. The difference is that these difficulties are more obvious in the indoor cat, who is underfoot much more often than an outdoor cat.

SET THE RULES

One way to prevent the onset of these behavioral problems is to combat them before they even have a chance to start. Knowing your cat and recognizing any behavior changes is very smart, but you can start even before that. When you first acquire a new cat, it is a good idea to set the house rules right off the bat. Cats are creatures of habit and abhor change. Most will reject any variation in their living pattern once that pattern is established, so setting a routine for your cat from day one will help prevent any problems later on. Before you even acquire your cat, you should know where your pet will be allowed, where she will eat each meal, where the litter box(es) will be kept, which counters are off-limits, which furniture she is or is not allowed on, and very importantly, where the scratching post will be located.

Even cats that have always been indoors can develop behavioral problems.

The highest incidence of behavioral problems occurs in cats that have been outdoors most of their lives and are then converted to indoor-only cats.

When you first acquire a new cat, it is a good idea to set the house rules right away. If your cat will not be allowed on the sofa...

PUNISH PROPERLY

Contrary to popular belief, cats *can* be trained. However, training cats is not the same as training dogs. Dogs are happy just to please us and will respond to a pat on the head and words of praise. Cats have a different level of thinking and require a different set of methods. One of the most important aspects in training a cat is *never* to hit or use physical force. Cats do not understand a harsh hand and will only resent and fear you, rather than learning what you are trying to teach them. If you wish to keep your cat away from a certain area, such as a table or countertops, buy a small squirt gun or spray bottle. A little squirt goes a long way. The only problem with this method, however, is that your cat may learn to anticipate the spray and thus avoid the area only when you are there. If this should happen, you can either keep your cat locked out of that room (which isn't always feasible), or you can place a deterrent in the location you want your cat to stay away from. Most cats don't like the feel of tinfoil or double-sticky tape under their paws and will quickly learn to avoid any surface covered with these substances. Pet stores and catalogs also sell mats that are made to deter pets from a chosen location with a mild electric shock.

...or the dining room table...

...and if you want her to use her scratching post, then you must make this clear with words and actions.

LOVE AND ATTENTION

Besides training your cat from the start, you will also want to make sure that kitty has plenty of love, toys, and interaction. A bored or lonely cat can be a destructive cat and may show her displeasure in any number of unattractive ways, such as biting, scratching, chewing the wrong things, bad eating habits, indiscriminate urination or defecation, or even over-grooming.

First of all, your cat should have a variety of toys to play with. Just giving her a catnip mouse every now and again is not enough. Cats, though they are believed to be such solitary creatures, do need plenty of interaction, and play is a great way to keep a kitty young and healthy. Fishing-pole-type toys are good interactive toys that cats absolutely adore. You can also try being creative and finding toys and games that your cat loves that are unique to you and her. Paper bags are an inexpensive yet well-loved toy for cats. We've all heard the expression "let the cat out of the bag." Well, your kitty might prefer to be let *in* the bag. Try dropping a catnip mouse into an upright paper bag and watch what happens.

Store-bought toys can also provide hours of entertainment, especially feathers and strings. However, when purchasing toys for your indoor cat, be careful of toys that have small parts glued on, such as bead eyes and string tails. Some cats, especially kittens, may actually swallow these and choke. Thin strings can get caught in a cat's intestinal tract. Use common sense when buying or making toys for your kitty.

If your cat shows signs of loneliness, getting another pet for her to play with may be just what she needs.

HOW TO MAKE A CATNIP TOY

1. Take a piece of untreated cloth (preferably a thick material) that is approximately 8" in length by about 8" in width. (You can make any size toy you prefer, cut into any shape you desire).
2. Fold the material in half, wrong side out.
3. Sew two of the sides, using only 1/4" seams, and then sew half of the third side.
4. Turn the material inside-out so that the correct side of the material is now on the outside.
5. Stuff the toy with good-quality dried catnip. You can also pack the toy with a durable, safe stuffing material so you won't need to use as much catnip.
6. Fold the edges of the remaining hole inward and sew close to the edge to close the hole. Back-stitch the seam to prevent unraveling as the cat plays.

GET KITTY A FRIEND

What if you play with your cat several times a day, yet she still shows signs of boredom or loneliness? If you are not home often enough to play with your cat, or if she needs more than you can give her, sometimes a companion is a solution to her dilemma. If your cat gets lonely and bored, she may take her

When purchasing toys for your indoor cat, be careful of toys that have small parts glued on, such as bead eyes and string tails. Some cats may swallow these or choke on them.

SIGNS SOMETHING IS WRONG:

- Aggression/Displaced aggression
- Biting
- Indiscriminate chewing
- Listlessness
- Loss of coat quality

What to Do:

- Make sure your cat is not lonely
- Plenty of exercise, toys, and interaction
- Lots of love, verbally and emotionally expressed
- Time alone
- Communication
- Proper nutrition and veterinary care

frustrations out in destructive patterns that can become very annoying to you. If she is a fairly social animal, she may love to have a new kitten or even a small dog to play with. Believe it or not, some cats love dogs; I have a dog-loving cat in my house. He rolls around in front of the dog, and they cuddle together at night.

Be careful when introducing two pets and take it slow, keeping them separated at first and then gradually bringing them together. Feeding them together sometimes helps to break the ice and gives them a positive association with one another right from the start. Watch dogs carefully. Some breeds have natural chase and prey instincts and may not be safe around cats.

Even if you have a cat that is king or queen of the house and refuses to allow another cat or dog in his or her territory, you can still get a companion to make the cat's days a bit less lonely. Fish tanks make wonderful little "televisions" for cats to watch. How about bird feeders outside the window? Contrary to what some may believe, cats that are intently watching birds outside the window are *not* wishing they were out there catching them. Cats simply do not think this way. Watching the birds or the squirrels outside a window is to a cat what being engrossed in a wonderful television program is to us.

TERRITORY DISPUTES

Rivalry between more than one cat in the same household is another dilemma faced by indoor cats, particularly in households with many cats. Two or three in a good-sized house, unless the cats have quite a personality difference, should not clash,

A bored or lonely cat may show her displeasure in any number of destructive ways. Plenty of love, toys, and attention can prevent boredom.

but six or more in a smallish house may. Feline rivalry is quite common and comes in various forms and degrees of severity. It may be as simple as one cat hissing at another as the other walks by or as complex as vicious tooth-and-claw fights every day. Jealousy, aggression, and displaced aggression (where a cat higher on the hierarchy of the house picks on a lower cat, who then takes it out on an even lower cat) are the most common characteristics of an unhappy cat. But this does not necessarily mean that you must find another home for one or more cats.

Cats are territorial animals, and clashes occur when one cat's territory invades another's. This is mostly a condition of overcrowding and can also be combated right from the start by making sure you don't acquire more cats than can comfortably fit into your household. I have heard "rules" of one per room, but this truly depends on the house and the cats in questions. Of course, some of us seem to attract every stray, and how can we turn them down? The result can be an overcrowded household, but fights don't have to be habitual.

There are several things that can be done without having to give up any of the kitties. How you go about handling disputes will depend on the severity of the situation. If the two cats are merely arguing over the mundane, such as who gets the last morsel of food in the dish, then separating the cats at mealtimes is in order. Separating the cats is also a good idea when a small spat occurs, such as a tiff over a particular sleeping location. Even as few as two cats in a household will develop a hierarchy in which one cat is "top cat" over the other. When one threatens another's position, the fur literally begins to fly.

Sometimes two cats simply cannot get along and fight every time they cross each other's path. In a

Believe it or not, some cats love dogs, especially if the two animals are raised together.

Placing bird feeders outside the windows of your home helps the birds and provides your indoor cat with some harmless entertainment.

CAT COMMUNICATION

Always ensure that your cat knows she is loved and that no matter what, you will work with the cat to solve any problems. A cat may not understand the spoken language of humans, but they do understand body language, thoughts, and emotions and will respond to them. Baby-talk your cat. They really do respond to this, and a soft voice will go a long way.

The proper love and communication as well as play, time alone, exercise, good food, and veterinary care will ensure your cat a healthy mind for all of her life.

severe case like this, there are several options. One is to separate the cats permanently into different parts of the house. This doesn't necessarily mean locking each cat into separate rooms. Keep the cats occupied with their "own thing" in different locations of the home. For instance, give them separate food dishes, litter boxes, scratching posts, and toys. Each cat will have her own territory away from the other. If it is feasible to keep them apart altogether, then do so, making sure that each cat has all the comforts and exercise required for a healthy and happy life. If you cannot keep them apart, then expect some spats to occur, but make sure each cat knows her own place. Play with each cat several times each day in her area to assure a positive association with that location.

Never acquire more cats than can comfortably fit in your household. Territorial aggression occurs when cats feel crowded or threatened.

Scratching

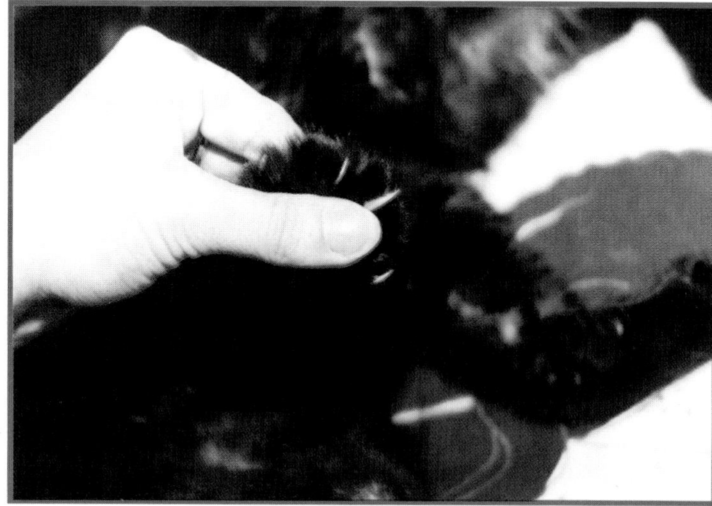

When cats scratch, they don't really "sharpen their claws." Instead, the outer sheath of the claw is sloughed off, leaving a fresh, sharper claw beneath.

The last thing you want is to have to give up your cat because she is destroying your furniture, and this does not have to happen. Cats can be successfully trained to keep their claws out of your furniture and to scratch an appropriate place of your choice instead.

In order to train your cat effectively, you must first understand the reasons your cat scratches. Cats don't destroy your furniture out of spite or for fun—they don't think that way. Actually, there are three very important reasons that cats instinctively use their claws. We've all heard that cats "sharpen their claws." This is only half true. What really happens when cats scratch is that the outer sheath of the claw is sloughed off, leaving a fresh and, thus, sharper claw beneath. You might notice something that looks like the cat's claws lying about on the carpet, but if you look closely, it is merely a hollowed-out shell that is shaped like the claw. This is the sheath.

Cats also scratch to mark their territory. This is very important to a cat and is an instinct that stems from the

You can, of course, have beautiful carpets and furniture *and* a cat, but your cat should be trained to scratch in appropriate places.

One important reason that cats scratch is to stretch the muscles in their back and legs.

Many people make the mistake of buying a scratching post that is too short for an adult cat—almost certainly guaranteeing that the cat will ignore it.

days when cats were wild animals. Though they are now fully domesticated, instinct still tells them "This area is mine now and I will mark it to show everyone else." On the bottom of their paws, cats have small ducts in the pads that contain scent glands. When the cat scratches, her scent is left behind, marking the area. You may not think your cat has a reason to mark her territory within your home, but she does. Single cats feel the need to establish territory among the humans in your house, and cats in multi-cat or multi-pet households declare their territory within the hierarchy of the other animals.

The third important reason cats scratch is to stretch the muscles in their back and legs. To a cat, there's nothing like burying those claws in a good, unyielding surface and having a good stretch. This activity is vital to the relaxation of muscles, especially when the cat has just awakened from a long nap. Though it may not be apparent to the owner, declawed cats do not get this benefit of claws and therefore can never really get that nice relaxing stretch. Owners of declawed cats can help a bit through massage.

With all these reasons, as well as some only your cat knows, it's more understandable why your kitty is destroying your sofa. But before you run out and get your cat declawed (which is definitely not recommended, especially for adult cats), know that understanding why cats scratch is only the first step in understanding how to solve the problems associated with scratching.

The first step in protecting your furniture is to buy a cat tree. It sounds simple (and it is), but there is more to it than that. You can go out and buy a cat tree with tiers

The first step in protecting your furniture is to buy a cat tree and place it in a location that is convenient and comfortable for the cat.

protruding everywhere, barrels for your cat to hide in, and strings with little balls on the end for your cat's batting enjoyment—but if you stick it in your basement or in a far-off room, you have wasted your money and your time. Your cat is not going to go searching for the tree when the sofa is right there, conveniently located for her scratching pleasure. On the other hand, you could go out and buy a small, carpeted post that practically tips over if your cat so much as walks past it and place it right next to your sofa. Once again, a waste of money and time. Your sofa is still full of claw marks, and you have spent hard-earned money on a cat tree or post your cat never uses.

The point of all this is that in order for your cat to give up scratching the furniture, you must provide a more satisfying alternative in a convenient location. Give your cat something more desirable than the sofa, and she will happily oblige.

The large, multi-tiered cat trees cost more, but cats prefer them to the smaller single posts. For some cats, a simple post may be enough, but in multi-cat households or for stubborn furniture scratchers, something more is in order. You want to steer your cat towards the appropriate scratching area. Since cats love high vantage points, a tall tree with many tiers or perches will provide more than just a place to sharpen those claws. Place the tree near the sofa or wherever your cat prefers to do the most scratching—in front of a window where the cat can watch the birds and squirrels is even better.

Cat trees come in many different types, sizes, shapes, and colors. You can even buy

In order for your cat to give up scratching the furniture and carpets, you must provide a more satisfying alternative.

Some cat trees are made of a combination of materials, including carpet, sisal rope, and natural wood. Cats love the different options.

All kinds of scratching post styles are available, including those that lie flat on the ground.

one to match the color scheme of your living room if you wish. But the most important aspect to consider is the material the tree is made of. Some are made out of carpet, while others are natural wood or untreated rope. You can also find trees that are made of a combination of materials. The latter is best for most cats because it gives them a good variety of scratching surfaces to choose from, which helps to alleviate boredom.

If you are talented and creative, you can make your own trees using any variety of materials. Be sure, however, that with any tree, the material is safe for cats and the tree base is wider than any other area on the tree to avoid having it tip over when the cat scratches it.

If your cat habitually scratches in different areas of the house or if you have more than one cat, buying more than one cat tree or several varieties of trees and sturdy posts will help solve the problem. Place them in the rooms where your cat scratches most often, near the furniture or area she claws at the most.

Of course, some cats may use the cat trees as a supplement to the furniture, scratching both. For this reason, just buying the trees is not always enough. You have to *train* your cat to use them. This is not as difficult as it may sound, but many people feel intimidated by the idea of training a cat and give up too soon. Again, the whole idea behind this is simply to make the appropriate scratching area more appealing than the inappropriate area. Pet stores

THE BEST CAT TREES ARE...

- Built with a wide base
- Made of a variety of materials
- Tall enough for the cat to be able to stretch
- Attractive to the cat as well as you

Some cats like scratching posts like this one that spin as the cat scratches.

SCRATCHING SURFACES THAT CATS LOVE

- Woven fabrics
- Corrugated cardboard
- Hemp
- Bark
- Untreated rope
- Carpet

sell plastic pieces that can be placed on the edges of the sofa legs where cats tend to do the most scratching. Cats hate scratching plastic. Tinfoil also works, as does double-sticky tape. The idea behind this is not to win the Ugly Furniture of the Year Award but to convince your cat that furniture is no fun to dig her claws into. Balloons can even be taped to the furniture so that when the cat scratches, the balloons pop, scaring the cat from the spot. If you catch your cat clawing in the wrong area, say "no" firmly. *Gently* take the cat's paws from the wrong spot and guide her to the tree (which should be very nearby). After a time, with patience, your kitty should get the idea.

Some cats don't need any training at all and will take to the cat tree immediately, all but forgetting the furniture. Others may need just a small amount of training, but still others need extensive reinforcement. Gear your training to the needs of your cat. Eventually, if training is done correctly and for a long enough period of time, the cat tree will be all your cats will scratch, and you can remove the plastic, tape, tinfoil, or whatever other deterrent material is plastered to your furniture.

DECLAWING

Unfortunately, not every method is foolproof, and sometimes a very stubborn cat comes along that thinks that the furniture is the best place for scratching, no matter what. Declawing is a very controversial option but is sometimes a better choice than getting rid of the cat. Essentially, declawing is the surgical removal of the claws as well as the last three toe bones and the cells that promote growth of the claws. The cat remains in the

If your cat persists in scratching the furniture, there are plenty of retraining methods you can try.

Eventually, if training is done correctly and for a long enough period of time, the cat tree will be the only thing your cat scratches.

hospital for a couple of days and comes home with sore, bandaged paws. This procedure, called onychectomy, should be performed as an extreme last resort if absolutely *nothing* else has worked.

Declawing is very extensive surgery that does not always have positive results. Because bones and tissue are removed, and the cat's paws are naturally very sore for quite some time after the surgery, some cats may avoid using the litter box even after the paws are healed. Other behavioral problems have been known to develop as well, and many cats that were declawed so the owner would not have to get rid of the animal have found themselves in shelters anyway because of the negative effects of the supposed solution to the problem.

Training your cat to use a scratching post is your best option for destructive behavior. Be sure to consult with your veterinarian about all other options before considering declawing surgery.

If you have not yet obtained a cat and are concerned about your furniture, you may be able to find a cat that is already declawed. A word of warning: A lot of declawed cats available through shelters are in the shelter because of behavioral problems caused by being declawed.

Besides declawing, there are other options. Keep your cat's nails trimmed short to help minimize any damage if your cat does scratch the wrong place.

You can also ask your vet about nail covers. These soft little vinyl caps fit tightly onto your cat's claws so scratching does no damage to your furniture. Nail covers are safe and painless.

While you and your cat work on these issues together, you will learn more about one another and develop a closer bond that will benefit you and the cat, not to mention your furniture.

Keep your cat's nails trimmed short to help minimize any damage if she does scratch in the wrong place.

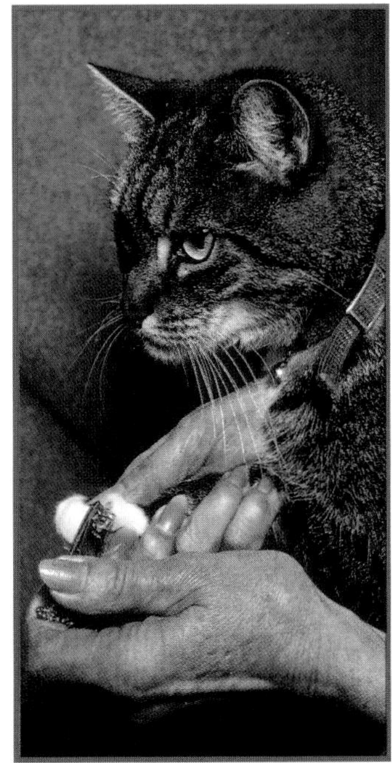

It simply isn't true that indoor cats spray all over the house. But when this does occur, it is easier for the indoor cat owner to diagnose and solve the underlying problem.

Litter Boxes

Not long ago, I heard somebody say, "I wouldn't keep my cat indoors. Indoor cats spray all over the house." Unfortunately, this is a common attitude among many outdoor cat owners. Fortunately, it's not true. Just like, "Indoor cats become fat and lazy," this is a myth. The truth is, outdoor cats actually spray more often because they are exposed to other cats and animals and feel more of a need to mark their territory, even the inside of their house. With indoor cats, the owner has an increased opportunity to learn why the cat is missing the mark and to prevent or solve this misbehavior. To truly understand the problem, let's start from the beginning.

CAT LITTER

The history of cat litter begins in 1947, when a man named Edward Lowe gave a bag of granulated clay to a friend for use in her cat's litter box. Up until this time, sand was used almost exclusively for pet cats. But sand, though natural, has no odor-eliminating abilities, is hard to clean, and is not very absorbent. The clay Lowe gave to his neighbor seemed to solve many of these problems, so Lowe placed his new product in bags and began to market it. He called it kitty litter.

Since that breakthrough, thousands of cat box fillers have been created from a variety of substances, from paper to clay to grass. With all the multitude of choices, how do you know which one to choose for your cat? Simple—let your cat decide. Every cat prefers a different type of litter. Studies have shown that most cats prefer sand-like box fillers and that the clumping clay litters are number one. Try many different types of litters, especially if you have a fickle cat that likes to avoid the box on occasion.

MISSING THE MARK

If your cat is avoiding the litter box regularly or just having that occasional accident, the following is a list of possible causes and solutions.

Until 1947, when cat litter was invented, sand was used almost exclusively for litter box filler.

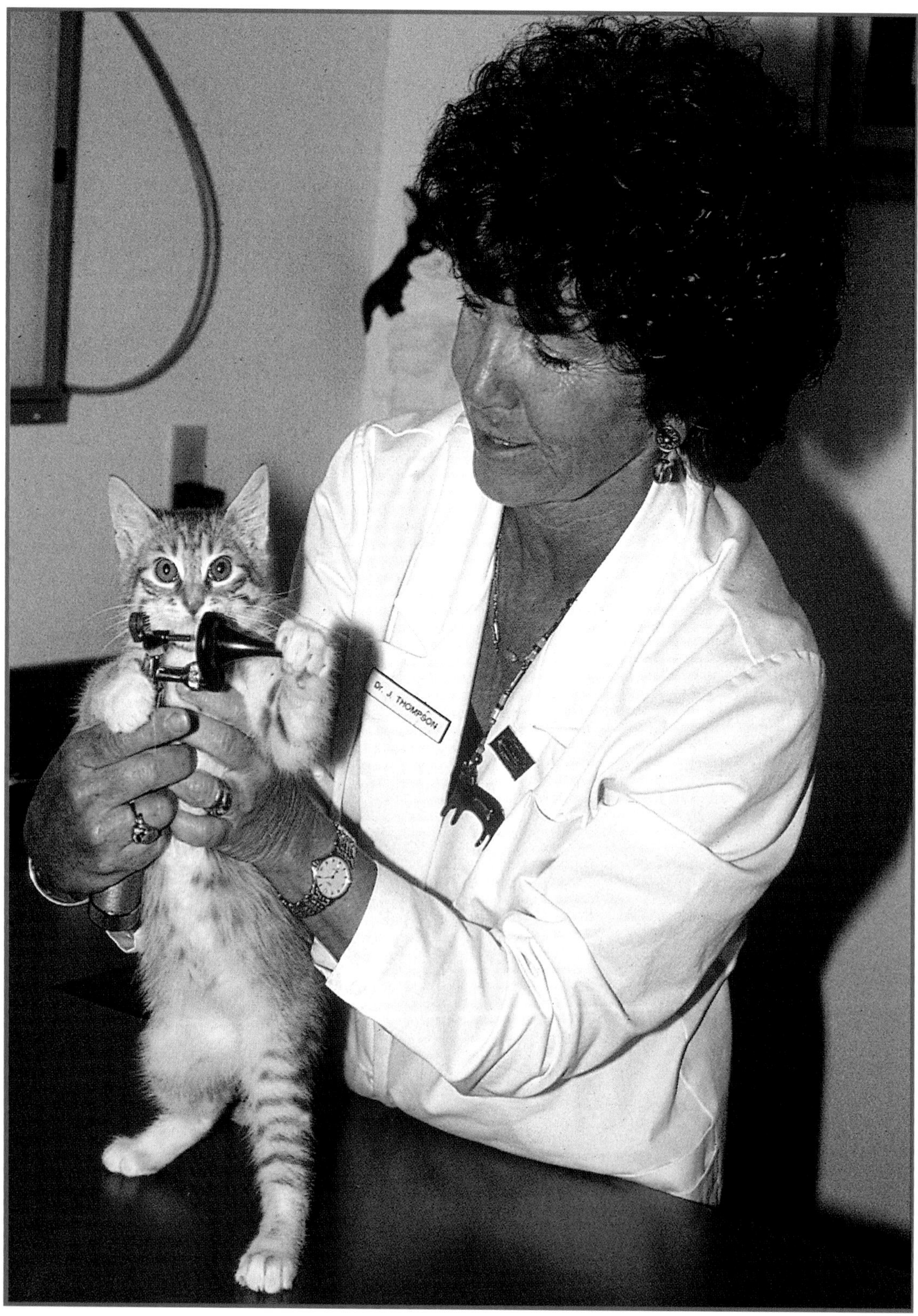

The first thing to do when litter box problems occur is to take your cat to the veterinarian for a physical examination.

Studies have shown that nine out of ten cats prefer clumping litter. This type of litter should never be used with kittens, however, because of the risk of ingestion.

Physical

Sometimes cats that are sick or in pain will shun the litter box, and once they associate the box with their illness or their pain, they may even avoid it after they get better. The first thing to do if your cat seems to dislike going in the litter box, especially if it came on suddenly, is to bring her to the veterinarian for a complete checkup. If the veterinarian gives her a clean bill of health, then something else is wrong and you will need to find out what it is.

Type of Litter

Some cats are just plain particular about the type of litter that you use. Studies have shown that nine out of ten cats prefer the clumping clay litters. However, just because your cat prefers clumping clay litter does not mean she will prefer every brand of that type of litter. Cats can be very fussy creatures, and many are especially fussy about the litter box. This is why it is a good idea to experiment with different types of litter and find one your cat will use consistently. Some cats may even prefer a combination of litters. For example, a good-quality clumping clay litter on the bottom and a cedar litter sprinkled on top will help keep the box clean as well as almost completely odor-free.

Litter Box

Sometimes the litter box itself is the problem. Some cats are not only particular about the type of litter that you use but also about the size and type of the box it is put into. If your cat is a young kitten or a very small cat and you have a large litter box with high sides, it may be difficult for the cat to climb in and out, so she will avoid it altogether. On the other hand, if the box is too small and your cat has trouble turning and scratching, she may also avoid the box or go over the side onto the floor.

The style of box is also a consideration. There are many different kinds of litter boxes, just as there are many different types of litter. There are covered litter boxes, nonspill litter boxes, self-cleaning litter boxes, and all types of regular plastic litter boxes. Some cats may oppose certain boxes, such as covered boxes, and some are afraid of the self-cleaning boxes. Make sure that the box fits the cat.

The material that the box is made out of is also something to consider. Most commercial litter boxes are plastic, but some people make their own out of wood or other materials that may be unattractive to the cat.

A dirty litter box can also turn a cat off, so make sure to clean it regularly.

Location

The location of the box should also be taken into consideration. If you have recently moved the litter box, your cat may go where the box used to be. In a case such as this, the box should be moved only a bit at a time to give the cat a chance to adjust slowly to the new location. Privacy is another factor. Just like you, cats tend to like to have privacy when they eliminate and often will not like their litter box to be in a place where there is high traffic. Privacy screens are available from pet stores and mail-order catalogs. Place the litter box in an area away from noise and heavy activity but not so far that the cat has to search to find the box. If you've recently acquired a cat, make sure that you show her exactly where the box is several times a day for the first few days until she knows for sure where to find it.

New Cat/Pet/Baby

If you've recently acquired a new cat or other new pet, your resident cat may be feeling a little rejected. Often, cats will show their dissatisfaction with a situation by avoiding the litter box. They cannot just tell you when they're upset. Also, a new baby can bring on feelings of neglect in your cat. If a newcomer has recently come into your household and your cat has stopped using the litter box, your cat may need more attention and playtime. Assure your cat that just because somebody new has come into the house, she's still number one and you still love her. Don't neglect your resident cat or cut back on her playtime and interaction—if anything, try to add more special times with you to her day.

Stress

Any number of factors can cause stress in your cat, and stress is one of the top reasons cats stop using the litter box. You will have to look around carefully to determine the cause of your cat's stress. Have you moved recently? Cats are creatures of habit and don't take well to their environment being altered drastically. There also may have been another cat or other pets in the house previously that your cat can smell, which makes her feel the need to establish her new territory. If you are moving, make the move less stressful for your cat by moving her last. Have everything in place before the cat comes into your new home. Make sure things are as close to the cat's previous environment as possible to try to keep stress levels minimal.

Cats generally prefer that their litter box be in a quiet, private location.

Sometimes a cat can get stressed out if her family is going on vacation. The hustle and bustle of packing and readying for a trip can cause quite a bit of stress in a cat. Some cats show their dissatisfaction by urinating or defecating in places they have not previously—even on your clothes or suitcase. To minimize the stress on your cat if you're taking a trip, try to pack early a little bit at a time during times when the cat is somewhere else or sleeping, not sitting and watching you pack. She will probably still know you're going away, but this may help minimize the stress involved.

Going to the veterinarian also causes stress. Not only is the trip itself stressful, but often if the cat comes back from the veterinarian and smells like the disinfectants and other animals she has encountered, another cat in the house may take offense to the smells and begin urinating indiscriminately.

Any number of factors can cause stress in your cat, and stress is one of the top reasons cats stop using the litter box.

Declawing

Declawing is a very stressful surgery that produces sore paws, and after the surgery, many cats will refuse to use the litter box because the sand-like litter hurts their sensitive feet. Special litters or shredded paper may reduce the amount of pain on the cat's feet and help prevent avoidance of the box.

Fear

A shy cat may not want to walk to the litter box if it is too far from her usual hiding place. If you have a shy cat, put the litter box near the place where she spends most of her time. Trauma that occurs in the box can also cause a cat to avoid the litter box. This includes such incidents as another cat scaring a shy cat while she is in the box, a loud noise, and similar events. The same is true for cats that are bullied by another cat. In multi-cat households, this can become quite common depending on how many cats are in the house. Cats form a hierarchy among themselves, and sometimes the top cat will bully a lesser cat if the lesser cat spends too much time in the territory the top cat has chosen. It may be necessary to keep cats that are lower on the totem pole and bully cats separated, with their own litter boxes.

Coming of Age

Spraying is another common form of indiscriminate urination. Cats that are five or six months old may be coming of age—females going into heat and males beginning to look for a mate. Make sure you have your cat spayed or neutered while he or she is young and preferably before the spraying behavior starts. This is not always possible, because some cats start early, but not waiting until the cat reaches full maturity will certainly help curb this behavior.

Competition

Again, in an overcrowded house with many cats or even many other animals, territorial disputes may arise.

This can lead to marking behavior as well as other problem behaviors. The best preventive medicine for this is to make sure that there are plenty of litter boxes for everybody and to make sure the bullied cat has a place to go where none of the other cats will bother her. Also, of course, don't overcrowd by taking on too many animals for the size of the house.

Liners

Some cats hate the liners that can be put into their boxes to make cleaning easier. Plastic liners crinkle when scratched, and a shy cat may be spooked by them. Other cats just may not like the feel of the liner under their paws. Try using the liners slowly at first, perhaps every other time you clean the box, and judge your cat's reaction. Use this reaction to decide whether or not to use the liners permanently.

Deodorizers

Cats have very sensitive nostrils. Their olfactory nerves are much more numerous than ours, which is one of the reasons they prefer to go in a clean box. Though deodorizers are made for the benefit of our limited smell, to a cat, being so close to the litter and having such heightened senses, additives may be overwhelming. As with liners, try using deodorizers only periodically until you are sure your cat does not mind them.

CLEANLINESS

It's important to keep the litter box spotless, and odor control is one of the most important aspects of the care of indoor cats. But simply scooping the box is not enough. The first thing to consider is how much litter you use in the box. If you use too much, the odor may build and have a chance to sit there longer; too little, and you will be scooping more than necessary. A good rule of thumb is to use about one-quarter to one-half the depth of the box.

Regularly disinfect the litter box and add fresh litter to help control odors. Even with clumping litters, scooping by itself won't keep the box odor-free forever. Bacteria builds up and gets trapped in the porous plastic of the box, and eventually, odors are trapped on the surface.

With most litters, the box should be dumped and

If you have a shy cat, place the litter box near where she spends most of her time.

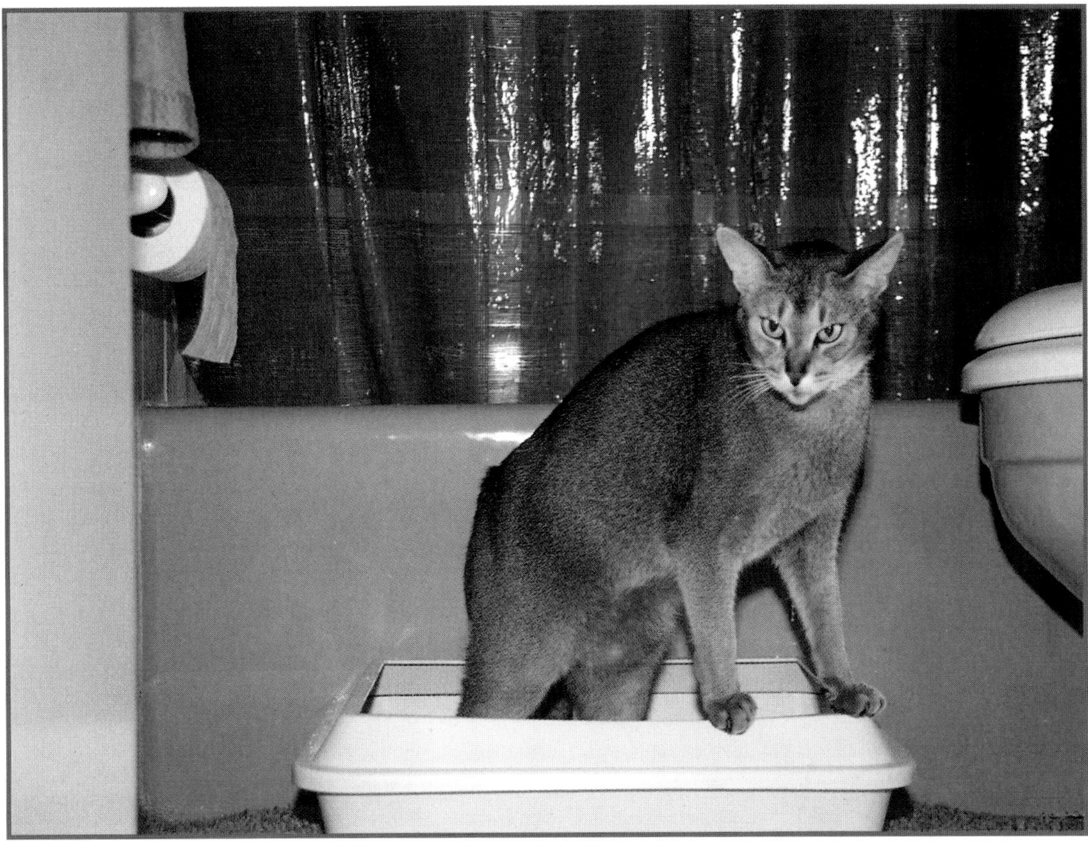

Cats have very sensitive noses, which is one of the reasons they prefer to go in a clean litter box.

disinfected at least once a week, preferably twice. If you use a good-quality clumping litter, every month or so should do the trick. If the box is not disinfected regularly, not only will odors become more penetrating and noticeable, but your cat has a higher risk of getting sick or contracting an infection from the bacteria buildup.

Make sure you sift the litter every time you scoop. This helps keep the litter dry, which is also important because moisture breeds the bacteria that cause odors and illness. Clumping litters are great because you can remove both kinds of waste rather than leaving the liquid behind. When scooping, make sure that you get to the bottom of the box by sifting thoroughly.

Even with continuous scooping, cleaning, and disinfecting, bacteria eventually builds to a point where it is difficult to clean out and odors linger or stains persist. When this happens, the only solution is to purchase a new box. It is good practice to try to replace litter boxes once every year or so, depending on the type of box you use.

Even with all your care, accidents can and will happen, whether because of one of the reasons already mentioned or because your cat has become ill. In any event, for odor control, the sooner you can get to the accident and clean it up, the better. Cats can smell things we can't, and any odor residue remaining in an area where a cat went to the bathroom will draw the cat back to that location, where there is a chance for recurring accidents. Use an enzymatic cleaner and allow it to soak into the area where the accident occurred, then blot it well to pull the odors out. A bleach-and-water solution will work well on linoleum, tile, cement, and the like—just be sure that all the bleach is thoroughly cleaned and dried before allowing your cat back to that location. Remember, if you can smell the bleach, so can your cat.

LITTER BOX TRAINING

Though kittens are trained

Mother cats train their kittens at an early age to use the litter box. However, you may need to train an orphan or a very slow learner.

at a very early age by their mothers to scratch and cover their messes (an ancient instinct that is believed to protect the cats from detection), you will need to train a very young kitten, one that's lost her mother, or one that just doesn't seem to know how to use the litter box. Consistency and patience are the keys to successful litter box training. This is also true when retraining a cat that has avoided the litter box for a while because of behavioral problems or illness.

The first step in training or retraining is to show or remind your kitten or cat where the litter box is. As mentioned earlier, you shouldn't place the litter box too far from where the cat spends most of her time, because many cats will find a more convenient place to go. Place the box in an area where the cat doesn't have to walk too far but that is private and out of traffic's way. Bring your pet to the litter box several times a day, reminding her where it is. Place her in the litter box and very gently guide her paws in a scratching motion.

If retraining a cat, it is especially important to associate the box with something positive. Giving treats near the litter box along with praise and love (especially if kitty does her business as she is supposed to) will help develop a positive association and reinforce appropriate behavior.

When retraining, be sure the problem that caused the indiscriminate urination is cured before working with your cat. Depending on the nature and extent of whatever caused your cat to stop using her box to begin with, you may want to try a few different methods for reinforcing a positive attitude. Place several boxes in different areas of the house, especially near the location of your cat's most frequent accidents. Then move the box a little bit each day toward your desired location.

If you see your cat using the litter box, praise her and make sure she knows she did well. Several times a day, remind your cat of the litter box locations by taking her to them and praising or playing with her—once again making sure of the positive association.

If you can't be home to supervise and your cat is not yet fully retrained, try closing her in a smaller area of the house with her food, water, and litter box.

Always use patience and kind words when it comes to training or retraining your cat in litter box duty, and never be harsh in any way. With persistence, she will get the hang of things and you will both be happier for it. Just remember, your veterinarian is always there to help if you need advice.

When you retrain an older cat to use the box, give her treats near the litter box along with praise and love to help develop a positive association in her mind.

Health and Grooming

Your indoor cat has a much longer average life span and is healthier than she would be if she went outdoors, but there will probably still be a time in her life that she will get sick. You should always know what to do to assure your precious pet's full recovery.

WATCH FOR CHANGES

For starters, know your cat well so that if something is amiss you will recognize the signs. Know how your cat not only looks but how she walks, what her fur feels like and looks like, how to look into her ears and check her eyes, and most importantly, how she normally behaves. Watch for any changes, such as listlessness or lethargy, and keep a close eye on your cat's appetite and eating habits. Especially with male cats it's a good idea to observe them in the litter box. If your cat seems to be straining or going to the litter box too often, it could be a sign of a urinary infection. This warrants an immediate veterinary checkup, because this condition can be fatal in male cats and quite uncomfortable for females.

Most cats vomit hairballs, food, or even bile sometimes, but if your cat seems to be vomiting too much and repeatedly, this is a sign that something might be wrong and also warrants a trip to the veterinarian. Gastrointestinal problems are commonly no more complicated than bouts of diarrhea, vomiting, or constipation. But occasionally, something more serious, such as a bowel, liver, or kidney infection or even tumors, can occur. Any sign of change in your cat's litter box habits should be checked by a veterinarian right away.

Cats can get depressed, so if you notice that your cat is moping about the house, she may be reacting to stress. Other important warning signs of various illnesses include increased thirst,

To monitor your cat's health, watch for any changes, such as listlessness or lethargy, and keep a close eye on your cat's appetite and eating habits.

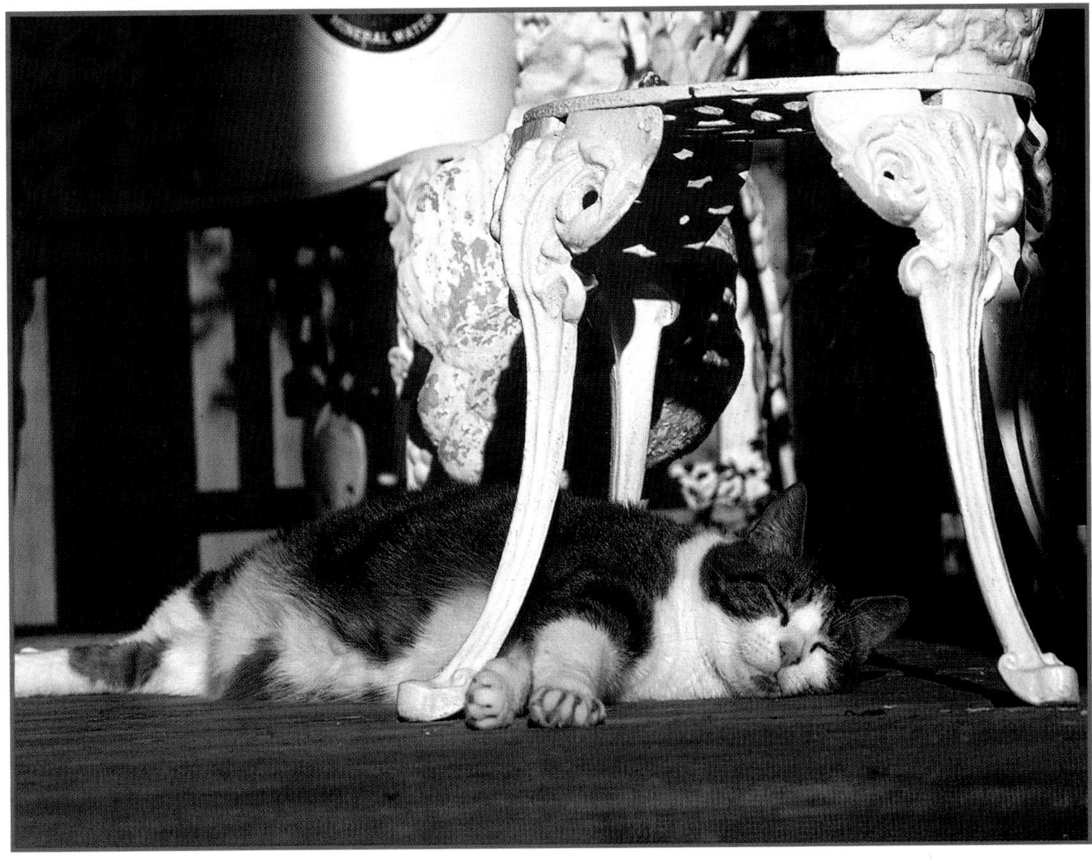

Keep your cat healthy by taking her to the veterinarian regularly.

SCHEDULE VET VISITS

Keep your cat healthy as well by making sure she makes regular trips to the veterinarian. There has been some controversy as to whether or not cats that are indoors need to have regular vaccinations. It is a good idea and often a legal requirement for your cat to be vaccinated against rabies. But vaccinating for distemper and respiratory infections can help prevent an indoor cat from becoming ill if she comes in contact with these diseases—either by someone carrying bacteria on their body, an animal coming into the house, or if she escapes. Some veterinarians only vaccinate indoor cats once every two years and once every three years for rabies. It's better to vaccinate once per year for the first five years to build up immunity and then once every other year after that. If you have a cat in your house that sneezing, coughing, respiratory problems, running eyes, or joint stiffness or lameness.

Get in the habit of checking your cat every day, and pay special attention to the areas mentioned above at least once a week to be sure that everything is all right and that there are no lumps, bruises, sores, or any other abnormalities beneath the fur. Check her ears and teeth and feel her body over carefully, including her feet. Make sure her nails are not too long or growing into the pads of her feet, which can happen with older cats that do not perform as much scratching as younger cats.

It's important to vaccinate your indoor cats once a year for the first five years of life and then once every other year after that.

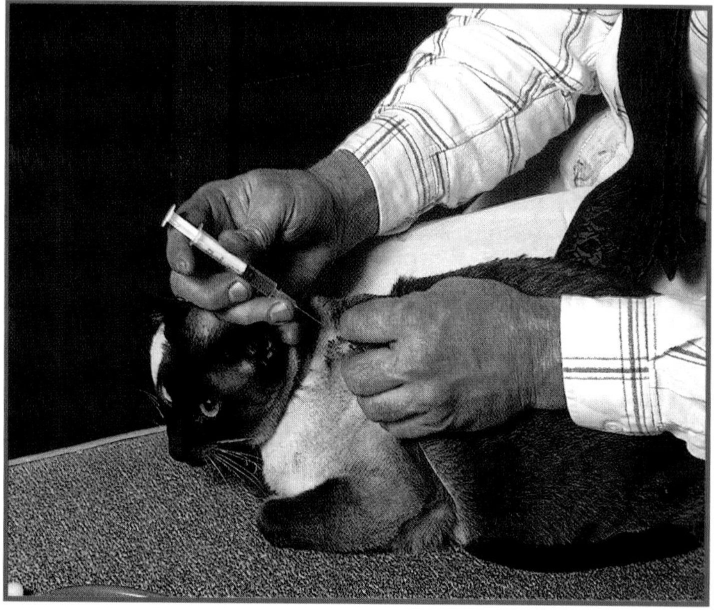

goes outdoors, the outdoor cat should be thoroughly vaccinated annually, and your indoor cats should also be provided the proper immunity.

MASSAGE AND EXERCISE

Massage is not only a good stress-reducer for humans but for cats as well, and the lowered stress will lead to better health. Most cats will relish the kneading of hands along their body. Use small circles, paying special attention to the back, neck, and shoulder muscles.

Be sure your cat gets plenty of exercise. Veterinarians will tell you that the proper amount of exercise can slow the aging process as well as provide cardiovascular health to the lungs, heart, and even bones. Exercise also reduces the stress that can cause health and behavioral problems. It is essential to provide your cat with plenty of playtime every day.

PARASITES

There are two types of parasites, internal and external. Internal parasites include worms such as *roundworms*, which are generally contracted either while the kitten is still in the womb or by eating rodents. Roundworms are very common in kittens and cause thinness with a potbelly, vomiting, coughing, diarrhea, and a dull coat.

Tapeworms are contracted by ingesting fleas from small mammals such as rats and mice. Segments of tapeworms are easily seen in the anal area of the cat and look a little bit like grains of rice.

Hookworms are generally contracted when the cat eats them or their eggs, which are often found in unsterilized soil. It's important to use store-bought potting soil in indoor plants because of the risk of hookworms.

To rid your cat of internal parasites, bring a stool sample to the veterinarian for tests. If it tests positive, the proper medicines in the right dosages will be prescribed.

Fleas are a common parasite even in indoor cats, but the new preventive flea medications make it possible to eradicate them entirely.

Massage is not only a good stress-reducer for humans but for cats as well.

External parasites are easier to detect than internal parasites. *Fleas* are the most common, and at one time or another most people have had problems with these little pests. Today, battling fleas is nowhere near the challenge it once was. At one time, the only way to deal with fleas was with expensive, messy, and potentially dangerous flea bombs, powders, sprays, and dips. But today there are breakthrough products that make battling fleas a winnable situation. These products are applied to the skin or given in food and are available through your vet or commercially, depending on the product. These products keep the fleas from being able to feed on your cat by killing them immediately so they never have a chance to breed and multiply. If you

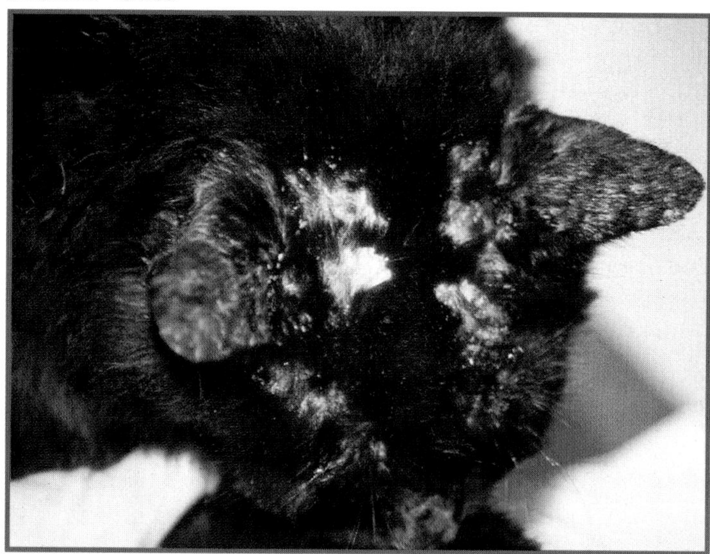

As seen here, ringworm manifests itself in cats as circular, hairless rings. This fungal infection is contagious to humans.

have no animals going in and out of the house and you only have one or two indoor cats, fleas will probably not be much of a problem. However, these pesky bugs can still hop a ride on you and other humans, so take precautions against them before they become a problem. Where there's one flea, there are thousands.

The next most common external parasite is the *tick*. These fat little bugs are not only annoying but can also transmit severe diseases such as Lyme disease and Rocky Mountain Spotted Fever. Some of the flea products kill ticks as well as fleas, but they must be applied every month without fail. Check your cat for ticks regularly, especially if you have other animals that go in and out of the house. If you find a tick on your cat, pull it off with a pair of tweezers, making sure that you get the entire tick and do not leave the head behind. Deer ticks, which cause Lyme disease, are very tiny and hard to detect. Signs of Lyme disease include stiffness in the joints, which is often confused with other ailments. If your cat seems sore and stiff, ask your vet to give her a Lyme disease test.

Other external parasites that can plague an indoor cat are *ringworm*—which is not a worm at all but a fungal infection—and *mites*. Ringworm shows itself as circular hairless rings and is contractable both to humans and from humans. Once diagnosed, it is easily treated in cats with medication or a lime-sulfur dip. On humans, it is treated with an antifungal ointment that can be purchased at the drugstore.

The most common type of mites that plague cats are *ear mites*. If your cat's ears look dirty, bring her to the veterinarian for a checkup, because she may have ear mites that will need to be treated with special drops.

Ear mites are very common in cats. If your cat's ears are filled with crumbly, brown, dirty-looking wax, have the veterinarian examine her for mites.

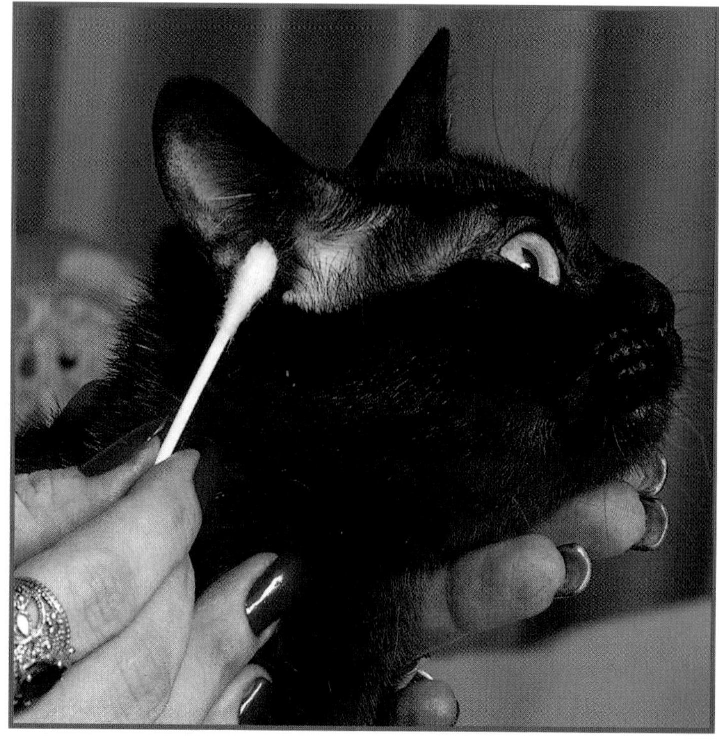

EMERGENCIES

Even in a controlled environment like your house, emergencies can and do occur. They are generally not as frequent or tragic as outdoor accidents but should be taken no less seriously. The first thing to remember is that if any accident occurs, get your cat to the veterinarian as soon as possible, even if the injury is not outwardly apparent. Internal injuries can be fatal. If your cat seems to be in shock, with symptoms like cold ears, hot or sweaty paw pads, fever, breathing trouble, or seizures, get her to the veterinarian posthaste.

Emergencies are tough because they happen so suddenly and often leave no room for reaction. Do not panic. Remain calm and use your head. Keep your veterinarian's day, night, and weekend numbers handy and learn who to call in case of an off-hours emergency. Call the veterinarian before you leave the house so that they will have someone there and be prepared to take care of your injured pet.

When handling an injured animal, be very careful, even with a pet that knows you well. When in severe distress and shock, even friendly animals may lash out. If she seems extremely agitated, use a towel to wrap the cat, keeping her paws (and thus her claws) in check. Talk softly to the cat and try to keep her calm. The calmer you are, the calmer your cat will remain.

If the cat is unconscious, first check her breathing and pulse. A cat's pulse can be felt on the inside of the inner thigh near the groin. An average heart rate is approximately 160 to 240 beats per minute. A heart rate that is too fast or too slow is cause for concern.

Move your injured cat very carefully so as not to aggravate her injuries. Use something as a temporary stretcher, such as a blanket or coat, or possibly a flattened box, board, or cookie sheet. If the cat has had a fall or been hit by a car, move the animal as little as possible when transporting her to avoid further injury.

Signs of shock include pale gums, rapid breathing and heart rate, confusion, and low temperature.

If the cat has swallowed a foreign object, tilt her head back and look down her throat, then very carefully remove any obstruction. Do *not* remove a needle or sharp object, because more damage can occur while you're trying to take the object out. Get the animal to a veterinarian immediately and let the professionals do it.

If the source of the injury is electrical shock, do not touch the electrical cord or the cat if the electricity is still live. Be sure to cut off the electricity first and move the cat away from the source. If you cannot cut the electricity, move the cat away using a wooden broom handle or other such object that does not conduct

If you suspect that your cat has swallowed a foreign object, tilt her head back and look down her throat, then very carefully remove any obstruction.

Many types of houseplants are poisonous. If your cat likes to nibble on your plants, make sure that they are safe.

electricity. Transport her to the veterinarian immediately.

Sometimes indoor cats get into household products that can poison them. Be very careful when dealing with household detergents, cleaners, and the like. Keep them capped and put away in a closed cupboard. Poisonous substances can be licked off of paws and even inhaled. If your cat is vomiting, coughing, having convulsions, seems to be in a lot of pain in the abdominal area, or is delirious, do not hesitate to get her right to a veterinarian. Bring a sample of the poison with you to the veterinarian if possible. This will help the vet determine exactly how to treat your cat for the best outcome.

Wounds, even small ones, should not be overlooked. Carefully clip the hairs around the wound with blunt-edged scissors to be able to see the area more clearly. Wash the wound with mild soap and warm water. If the wound is minor, apply hydrogen peroxide to kill bacteria. Watch the wound carefully for the next couple days and if it becomes red or swollen, get the cat to the veterinarian. If the wound is large or will not stop bleeding, do not hesitate to seek help.

If your cat is burned, place cold packs on the area and bring her to the veterinarian. Do not apply any kind of ointment. If the burn is very minor, apply an ice pack for 15 minutes several times a day and watch the wound carefully for signs of infection.

If your cat seems to be in respiratory distress, is pawing heavily at her mouth, has a pale tongue, or is unconscious, she may be choking. This is a true emergency and your cat will need help immediately. Remove any object that is obstructing the airway, again with the exception of needles or sharp objects that could cause more harm. If the object cannot be removed, you can try forcing it out. Very carefully set the cat on her side and place your palms behind the ribcage on both sides of the abdomen, then press your palms together several times, thrusting firmly. This should be done if possible while you are transporting the cat to the veterinarian. If you're alone and cannot dislodge the object yourself, rush the cat to help.

Homes with indoor cats should have secure screens on every window. Cats are rumored to be very surefooted, but many cats have been killed from falls out of upper-story windows, especially from high-rise apartment buildings.

POISONS FOUND IN THE HOME

Insecticides
Rat and mouse poisons
Antifreeze
Fertilizers
Herbicides
Chemicals
Plants
Human medicines
Dangerous foods (such as chocolate)

GROOMING

More than likely, your cat will never need a bath. Because she is not exposed to dirt, grime, oil, or other substances that can be found outside, her coat will be much cleaner and softer than an outdoor cat's coat. However, there may be an occasion

Before bathing your cat, clip her nails to prevent damage to you during the bath.

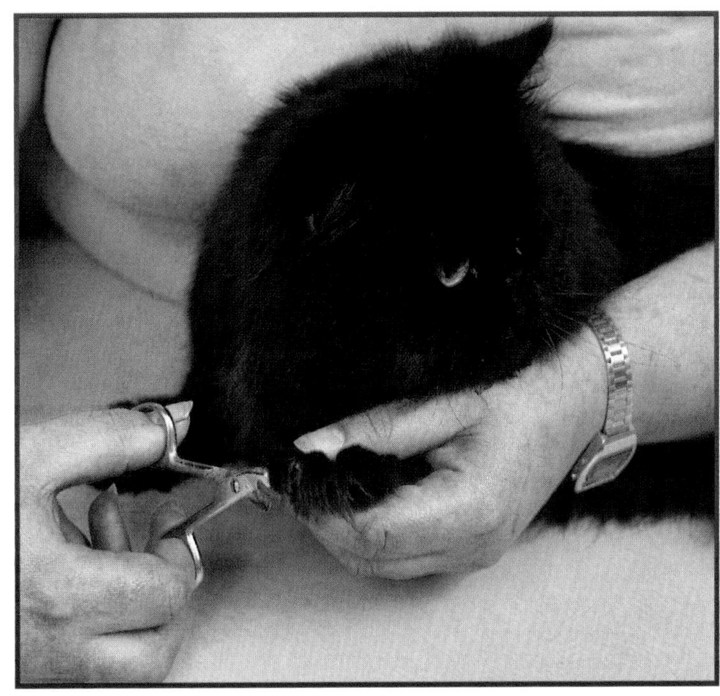

Most short-haired cats love to be combed, although this is not absolutely necessary for a healthy coat.

Bathing a cat is not always a pleasant task for cat or owner.

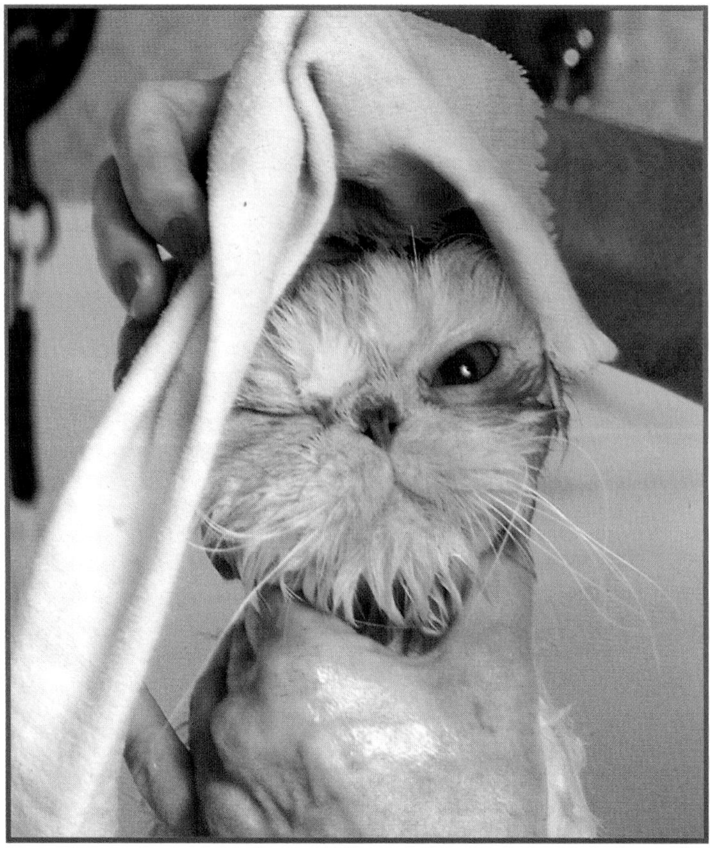

when your indoor cat gets into something that must be washed from her fur. If she gets into something that could poison her if she licks her fur, you will want to wash it out.

Bathing a cat is not always a pleasant task. Most cats, especially those that were not bathed regularly since they were kittens, will hate the idea. If you absolutely need to bathe your cat and for whatever reason cannot get her to a groomer, follow these steps.

First, clip her nails. This will help prevent damage to you during the bath. Get your cat into a position that allows you control and is also comfortable for you as well as the cat. Clip the nails by carefully squeezing one paw until the nails are extended. Clip only the part of the nail that curves, being careful not to clip into the quick (the pink vein running along the inside of each claw). Most cats are all right with having their nails clipped so long as it is done from kittenhood and they have grown used to it. As with all aspects of training a cat, you will have the best results if you associate the nail clipping with positive rewards.

Make sure everything is ready for the bath before you bring in the cat. Use a cat shampoo, because human shampoo can dry the cat's skin and coat. Also set out a towel, washcloth, and a couple of plastic cups. Draw the water and fill the sink halfway with warm water. Have the shampoo ready, cap off. If possible, have someone help you. Bring in the cat and set her carefully into the water, speaking very calmly and trying to keep her from getting too upset. If she absolutely will not accept the bath without shredding you to pieces, but there is something in her fur that needs to be washed out immediately, try getting her to a groomer. If that is not possible, you may want to do a spot-washing by holding her in your lap or in a comfortable location away from the water and using a bucket and washcloth to wash the substance carefully from her fur.

If she allows you to bathe her, make sure that you rinse the soap out very well and then wrap her carefully in a big, fluffy towel. Do not allow her near a draft until she is completely dry. You can use a blow dryer as long as she allows it, being careful not to hold it too close to her skin and keeping it on a low setting.

Grooming the Long-Haired Cat

Unlike short-haired cats, long-haired cats need regular grooming to keep their coats beautiful. If possible, start when the cat is a young kitten, getting her used to the feel of the brush and the attention. A wire-toothed slicker brush works well on thick coats. These can be bought inexpensively at any pet store and do a good job when used regularly. Brush your long-haired cat every day and use a close-toothed comb a couple of times a week. When brushing, be careful not to pull at any mats that you find; instead, try to work the mat out carefully by holding it near the skin as you brush. If it is a tough mat, you can use blunt-edge scissors or clippers to remove it, being careful not to clip the skin. Make sure that when you brush your cat, you part the fur and brush down to the skin, combing out the under–coat as well as the overcoat.

Keeping your cat brushed will not only benefit her coat but will help prevent hairballs from forming in her stomach when she bathes herself. With plenty of daily care, keeping toxic substances out of harm's way, and making sure your cat's coat is healthy and luxurious, you will have a cat to be proud of for many years to come.

Long-haired cats like this Persian need regular grooming to keep their coats beautiful. Brushing, combing, and bathing will all be easier if the grooming begins in kittenhood.

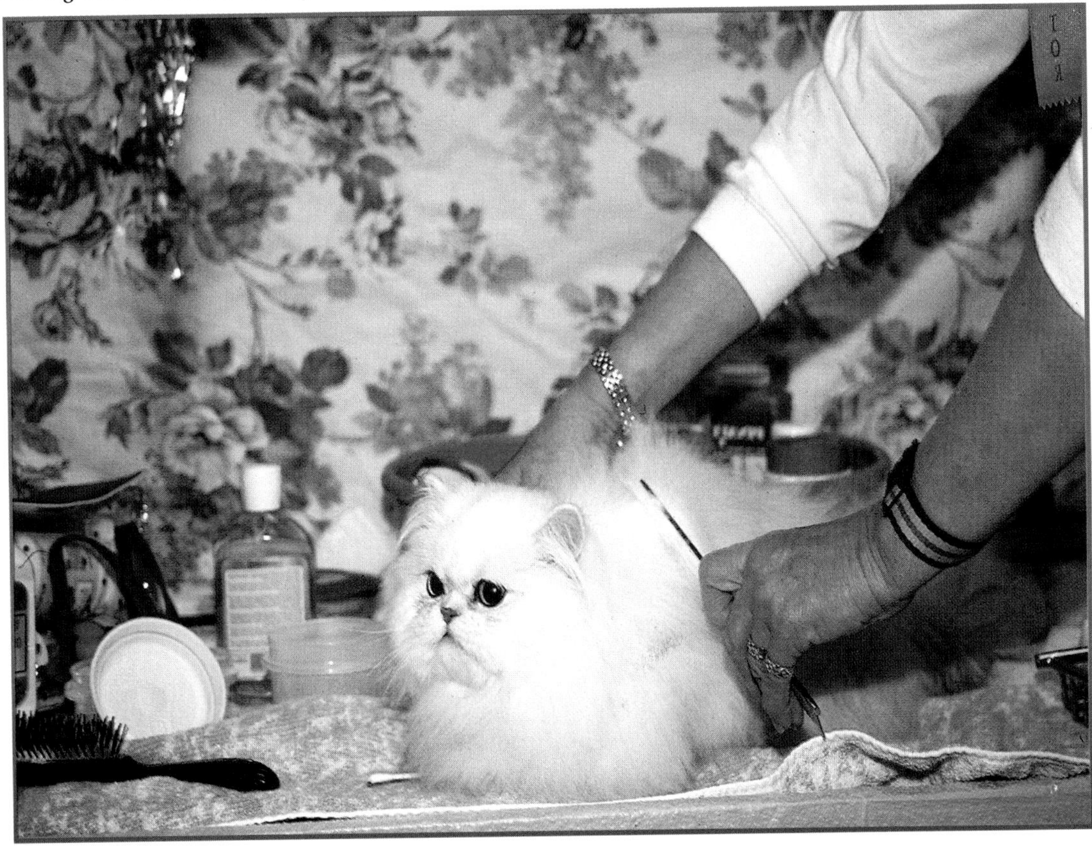

Nutrition

The old adage "you are what you eat" is generally associated with humans but can apply to cats as well. Just like you, your cat will benefit from a well-balanced diet.

Cats are carnivores and require meat to survive. A necessary part of a cat's diet is taurine, which is found in red meats. Without taurine, your cat would develop deficiencies of necessary vitamins and become ill. Cats require food that is rich in protein, with the right amount of fat, minerals, vitamins, and carbohydrates. If you buy commercial food for your cat, make sure the label states that it is 100 percent nutritionally complete and that the food conforms to the recommendations of the AAFCO (Association of American Feed Control Officials).

Feeding a varied diet of nutritional foods will not only ensure your cat's health but help prevent a finicky appetite. Don't feed her just meat or just fish, but a combination of flavors. Commercial foods offer the best variety. If you choose to make your cat's food yourself, be sure your recipe contains the proper amount of taurine, protein, vitamins, etc. A diet containing only fish or tuna will cause a Vitamin E deficiency, endangering your cat's health. Feeding your cat a combination of dry and moist foods and providing a constant supply of fresh water will assure the maximum amount of nutrients and liquids.

FEEDING TIME

So, how much should you actually feed your cat? Kittens eight weeks to four months of age should be fed two or three meals per day of a good-quality kitten food. Adult cats are generally fed two meals per day. If your cat is not prone to gorging herself and overeating, then it is all right to keep a dish of dry food down at all times for the cat to snack on. If your cat does tend to eat too much, leaving food out all the time will only create an overweight kitty. Feed an overeater just two

Kittens eight weeks to four months of age should be fed two to three meals per day of a good-quality kitten food.

Do you have a tubby tabby? The way to tell if your cat is overweight is to try to feel her ribs—if you can't, then she is too fat.

regular meals a day. You can even supplement the dry food with some moist food as long as you do not over-feed your cat.

We've all heard the rumor that housecats become fat and lazy, but this does not necessarily have to be the case. Once a cat is neutered or spayed, his or her metabolism does slow, but as long as you adjust the diet to compensate for this, you should have no problems (unless your cat has a thyroid or other medical condition).

DO YOU HAVE A TUBBY TABBY?

The way to tell if your cat is overweight is by feeling her ribs. If you can feel them but they do not protrude, then she is of the correct weight. However, if you cannot feel the ribcage under her fur, there is a good chance your cat is overweight and needs a diet.

If this is the case, especially if the weight came on suddenly, have your veterinarian give her a full checkup before you assume she is overeating. A thyroid condition could cause sudden weight gain. If she is given a clean bill of health, it may be time to change her diet or cut back on the food that you are currently feeding her.

Prevention is the best method—being careful that your cat does not become overweight from the start. Feed her good-quality food in measured proportions that are correct for her size and activity level (consult your veterinarian). If you see her gaining weight, cutting back on her food should do it. If your cat is already well on her way to being overweight, you will not only have to cut back her food but also increase her activity with more play and feed a lower-calorie diet. Obesity, just as with humans, can cause many health problems and shorten your cat's life. If your cat is

Medical problems may be the cause of finicky eating habits, so have your cat examined by a veterinarian if she turns her nose up at the food you offer.

Finicky eaters can be a tough challenge for their owners, although few cats will actually allow themselves to starve even if they don't like a particular brand of food.

grotesquely overweight, check with your veterinarian about a proper diet and feeding schedule.

FINICKY FEEDERS

Some cats don't want to eat anything you put in front of them. These are the finicky eaters. Most cats will not starve to death if you simply leave food out for them at all times. They will eventually eat it, even if they only pick little bits at a time. However, in rare instances, cats can develop a form of anorexia nervosa, so if you suspect your cat is not eating properly, see your vet before it becomes a problem. Cats can develop finicky eating habits if their owners change foods too frequently, feed only one flavor or type of food all the time, or cater to their pets' whims excessively. Some cats, however, are just plain finicky. Finicky eating habits may have an underlying cause such as a medical problem, which should be diagnosed by veterinarian. A change of food can sometimes cause a cat to turn her nose up as well. In this case, try changing the food over slowly by mixing the new food with the old food, gradually adding more of the new and less of the old. Some medications may also cause finicky eating, so check with your veterinarian if your cat is on medication. Cats often won't eat cold food, so any food coming out of the refrigerator should be heated to room temperature before feeding. Even the type of food dish you use can make a difference to some cats. Be sure the dish is clean and the cat is able to eat from it easily.

TIDBITS AND TIPS

Feed your cat in the same place every day, and if you have more than one cat, you may want to feed them separately to avoid one cat stealing from the other's dish. Cats do not like to eat near where they eliminate, so keep food dishes and litter boxes separate. Ceramic or stainless-steel dishes are preferable to plastic dishes, because some cats have allergies to plastic. Also, plastic is more porous and collects bacteria more quickly. Food bowls should always be washed between meals.

Make sure your cat has fresh, cold water at all times, especially in the summer when it is hot. Change the water at least twice a day, making sure you wipe or wash the bowl thoroughly before refilling.

If you have more than one cat, you may want to feed them separately to avoid one cat stealing from the other's dish.

Milk can be given to your cat as a treat. However, adult cats are often lactose-intolerant and will develop diarrhea from too much milk, so only give small amounts at a time. Plain yogurt can also be given as a treat. Never give a cat alcohol or anything alcohol-based.

Be careful with table scraps. A few bites of meat or vegetables once in a while is fine, but feeding too much can result in obesity or inadequate nutrition. Never feed your cat sweets or candy—especially chocolate, which can make your cat very ill.

Make sure your cat has fresh, cold, clean water at all times. Some cats even love to drink from a running faucet.

Although cats are carnivores, a little green roughage can be a good addition to their diet. Cats naturally eat grass to aid their digestion, and the indoor cat does not have to be deprived of this treat. You can grow grass in pots or buy a cat garden kit at the pet store. This also helps keep your cat away from your houseplants.

As long as you feed your cat a diet that is nutritionally complete, there should be no need for supplements, unless directed by your veterinarian. Remember that what goes into your cat makes quite a difference to her health and longevity, so feed her properly—and don't forget the occasional kitty treat.

Milk may be given to your cat as an occasional treat. However, adult cats are often lactose-intolerant and will develop digestive problems from too much milk.

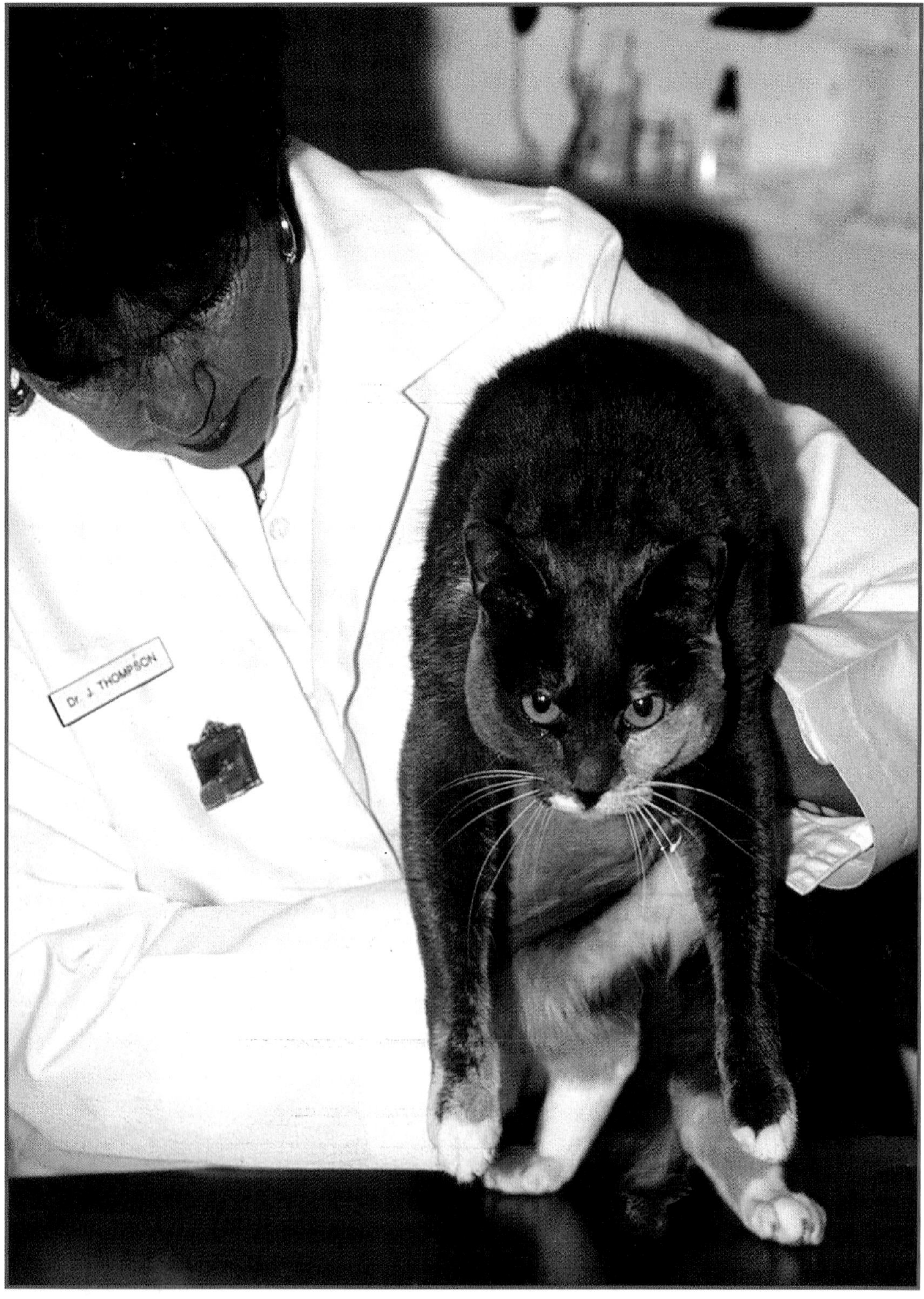

Aging cats should have regular veterinary checkups so that any problems that crop up are caught before they become serious.

Old Age and the Indoor Cat

Your indoor cat is healthier and confronts less danger than her outdoor counterparts. Therefore, she may live much longer than they do, maybe even exceeding 20 years of age—not uncommon for indoor cats.

Aging cats should have regular veterinary checkups so that any problems that crop up are caught before they become serious. Just like humans, aging cats develop physical infirmities and need more care to keep them going. Your cat's body is changing, and this change can affect almost any organ in the body. The most common geriatric problems seen in cats are bowel dysfunctions, diarrhea, constipation, and incontinence. Hearing and eyesight may also fade. Cats that have trouble seeing cannot judge distances and may miss jumps or fall while climbing stairs. Cats that cannot hear will not know if danger is approaching them from behind. If you suspect your cat is losing or has lost her eyesight and/or hearing, take steps to ensure the cat's comfort and safety by removing any dangers, such as obstacles a blind cat might run into. Blind cats will usually learn their way around quite nicely as long as everything is kept in the same place.

Older cats sometimes develop cataracts, which make the eyes appear cloudy.

Older cats sometimes develop cataracts, which make the eyes appear cloudy. Graying fur and a dull coat are also not uncommon. Don't neglect your cat's regular grooming, because her diminished mobility may

***Following pages:* Your older cat deserves to be happy in her twilight years, so do your best to please her—giving her more or less attention as she prefers.**

Obesity is a concern for some older cats. Adjust the cat's food intake accordingly.

prevent her from grooming herself as she once did.

Watch your cat more closely and continue to check her regularly. This is the time in your cat's life when more ailments will rear their ugly heads. Arthritis, joint stiffness, flabby muscles, and decreased activity are all common in the aging cat. Geriatric cats are also more susceptible to disease and may get chilled more easily than a younger cat.

Older cats often lose weight, and this is fairly normal, but watch that your cat does not lose too much weight because this may indicate a problem such as a thyroid condition. Obesity is also a concern of some older cats. Adjust the cat's food intake accordingly. Older cats can sometimes become finicky because their sense of smell is not as acute as it once was. Gum disease is also very common and your aging cat may actually lose her teeth. If this happens, make sure to feed her foods that she can eat, such as moist or semi-moist foods.

Consult regularly with your veterinarian and make sure any cat ten years of age or older has a full geriatric checkup, including bloodwork, at least once per year. Diseases that are most common to the geriatric cat include diabetes and hyperthyroid conditions.

As cats grow older, they sometimes become ornery and may not like to be petted as often as they did when they were younger. On the other hand, some cats go in the opposite direction and want to be cuddled more than they did before. Your older cat deserves to be happy in her twilight years, so do your best to oblige her.

Litter box habits are also affected by age. Many older cats develop urinary deficiencies, and it is not uncommon for an aging cat to stop using the litter box altogether. You may want to provide her with more litter boxes in different places, or you can also confine her to a smaller section of the house, as long as this does not upset her and she's still able to get the exercise she needs.

Make sure your older cat's claws are not growing too long. Less scratching activity, which is often seen in older cats, can

If your aging cat loses her teeth due to gum disease, feed her moist foods that she can eat easily.

cause the claws to grow too long and curl until they are actually growing into the bottom of the cat's foot pads. Clip your cat's nails or have them clipped regularly—once a week or once every other week.

Sadly, you will eventually have to say goodbye to your precious friend. When this happens, remind yourself that you gave her the best possible life that she could have had. Surround yourself with friends who understand and who will not belittle you for your feelings of grief over your cat's passing. Give extra attention to your other pets. Wait as long as you need to before acquiring another cat, but don't feel guilty if you want to get a new cat right away. After all, your heart holds plenty of room for more.

Many older cats develop urinary deficiencies, and it is not uncommon for an aging cat to stop using the litter box altogether.

Your indoor cat may live as long as 20 years before slowing down with age.

CAT/HUMAN YEARS

Below is a chart to determine your cat's age in human years. On the left is the cat's age, and on the right, the human equivalent. The old adage "One year of a cat's life equals seven of a human's" is false.

Cat Years:	Human Years:
1	15
2	24
3	28
4	32
5	36
6	40
7	44
8	48
9	52
10	56
11	60
12	64
13	68
14	72
15	76

Escaping

Quite a few years ago, I had a terrifying experience when one of my indoor cats escaped. The back screen door did not close properly when my brother went out one day, and the door stuck to the porch ceiling at the top, holding the door open about eight inches. Though most of my cats are too frightened of the unfamiliarity of the outdoors to try to get out, this was too much of an invitation to resist for my cat, Taffy, who had an adventurous nature. When I came home later that day, I could not find Taffy anywhere, and I began to panic. I remembered that the door sometimes did not close all the way, and my brother informed me that the door had indeed stuck open for a short time that day.

I searched the house thoroughly and waited until after suppertime just in case she was hiding in the house somewhere, but in my gut I had a bad feeling that turned out to be correct. Taffy had gotten out!

Though most of the author's cats are too frightened of the unfamiliarity of the outdoors to try to get out, Taffy couldn't resist the temptation of an open door.

I questioned the neighbors first, and one said she had seen a cat heading towards the woods in back—a cat she did not ever remember seeing before. I knew this had to be Taffy, and so I started the search. Several friends helped me search the woods, calling her name and opening cans of cat food and tuna fish. I went from door to door and handed out my phone number. I also made up signs to post around the area. I hoped she had not traveled to the nearby main road, where I had lost cats years ago before I began to keep my pets indoors.

I did not find Taffy in the woods, nor did any of my friends find her. The next day, I noticed that some plants on the porch were tipped over. Because I had no other cats that went out there, I assumed that Taffy had come around during the night and tried to get in.

My friends and I formed another search party for her the next day but again did not find her. The second night came, and once again I had not found my indoor cat. Fortunately, the elements were on my side and I did not have to worry about her getting caught up in inclement weather. I did, however, worry about *everything* else, because this cat had never been outside and an indoor cat roaming for the first time can get into much danger.

About 2 a.m. the second night, I rose from bed because I could not sleep due to my worry. I looked outside—and

The author and her friends left out cans of cat food and tuna fish, but Taffy was nowhere to be found.

there was Taffy sitting on the back steps waiting to be let in, as if this were something she did every day.

PREVENTION

Fortunately, my story had a happy ending. But that may not always be the case if your indoor cat has the urge to escape. Rather than waiting for this to happen to your cat, you can prevent it from happening in the first place.

Start by walking around your house and looking for any openings your cat could possibly escape through, such as screens that are not secure enough, doors that do not close properly, holes (perhaps a chimney or old smokestack) that are not properly closed up, or any other area that a cat could squeeze through.

Make sure that you inform anyone coming in and out of your house that you have indoor cats and that they must be sure to close the doors behind them when they come in or out. This also includes children. If you have kids, be sure to teach them to close the doors behind them, especially doors that have tight springs or do not close quickly. Some cats are very good escape artists and will dart for a closing door. Be sure that if your cat does have a habit of trying to get out as the door is closing, she does not get trapped in the door and injured.

ESCAPES

You may want to provide your pet with some form of identification to wear at all times, especially if you live in a house with a lot of in-and-out activity. This way, if your cat does happen to get out and disappear, someone finding her will know where she is supposed to be.

Collars and Tags

The most common form of identification is a collar and ID tag. These can be purchased in a pet store, ordered by mail, through your veterinarian, or even at a do-it-yourself machine found in some department stores or pet shops. Make sure that at least your name and phone number and preferably your address as well are on the tag. If you can, place any pertinent medical information as well as the fact that your cat is an indoor cat on the back of the tag.

Never put a tag on a flea collar. The collar should preferably be made of nylon or a soft material and should be expandable so that it will come off if your cat gets caught on a branch or bushes. If you plan to use a collar and tag as identification for your cat, try to teach the cat to wear a collar while she is still young. Adult cats often will reject having something put around their neck if they never had anything there before, and it can be difficult to train an older cat to accept a collar. Some cats may oppose a collar so adamantly that they hurt themselves trying to get it off.

Rabies tags can also be used as a form of identification, and in some states where rabies vaccinations are the law, it is good practice to have a rabies tag on your cat if there is a chance she could get out.

Although collars and tags are the most visual form of identification, they have quite a disadvantage in that they can be removed or fall off.

Two days later, there was Taffy sitting on the back steps waiting to be let in, as if this were something she did every day.

Tattoos

Another form of identification, more common with dogs than cats, is a tattoo. Generally, tattoos are placed in the groin region and sometimes in the ear. The problem with tattoos is that first, people do not normally know to look for them and second, they are hard to see once the hair grows back over the area where the tattoo is. They can also be removed, which happens occasionally with kidnapped purebreds.

Your cat must also be registered with a tattoo registry, so whoever finds your lost cat must know where to call. Unless a shelter with knowledge of tattoos finds your cat, the chances are that the tattoo will not even be noticed. Cats that are registered with tattoo registries are issued a tag to place on their collar with information about the animal and the fact that it is a tattooed animal. But, once again, if the tag gets lost many will not know the cat is tattooed. Some people who tattoo their pets keep the area around the tattoo shaved so that the tattoo is always noticeable. Tattooing can be done at clinics, through your veterinarian, through dog trainers, or through groomers.

Microchips

In this day and age, new technologies are helping to

You may want to provide your indoor cat with some form of identification to wear at all times, especially if she is an escape artist or is trained to walk on a leash.

Try to think like your cat when you look for her. Cats like small and high spaces, so check in bushes and trees.

identify lost animals and return them to their owners. Microchip implants are the new wave in the technology of lost pets. A tiny chip is injected into the pet, generally between the shoulder blades, which contains a registration number. These are decoded in exactly the same way that scanners in stores read bar codes. More and more shelters are equipped with the proper scanners needed to read microchip implants, and it is becoming common practice to scan pets automatically that are brought in. However, if a neighbor or other regular person finds your cat, they obviously cannot scan the cat to find out who the owner is.

Microchip implants like this one, encoded with identifying information, are the new wave in the technology of lost pets.

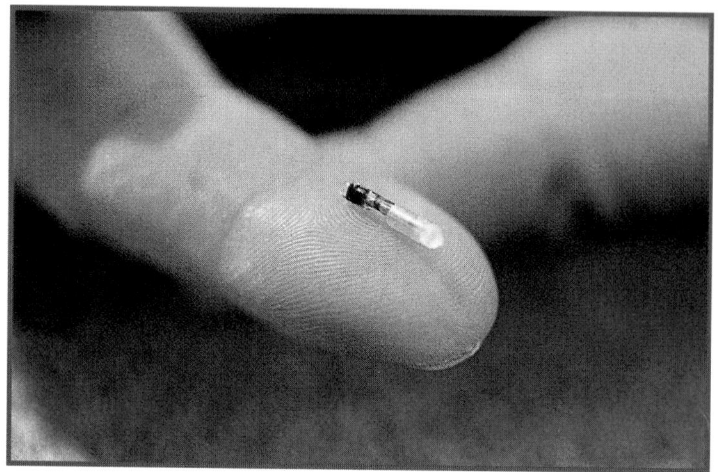

WHAT TO DO AFTER AN ESCAPE

But what if your cat does get out and you are not able to find her easily? What do you do then? Well, first of all, don't panic. Check the house thoroughly. Has something recently frightened your cat, a new person in the house for example, that may make her

If your indoor cat has escaped, don't panic. She may not have gone far—cats will often find hiding places that we humans have no inkling of.

Wherever she is, your cat may be so frightened that she *wants* you to come and rescue her.

want to hide away? Often cats will find hiding places that we humans have no inkling of. For example, we have a hole in the ceiling of our basement that the cats have sometimes managed to get up into. If you can't find your indoor cat, she just may have found one of these out-of-the-way napping places. Walk around the house, calling her name and using food or something else that makes a sound or smell she will respond to. Some cats wake at the sound of a can opener or a rattling toy. Especially if you live in a high-rise apartment or other place where it may be close to impossible for your cat to have gotten out, be sure to search thoroughly or wait a day and see if your cat materializes on her own.

Widening the Search

Has a window or door been opened recently that she may have slipped through? If you are sure she is not in the house, continue your search outside. Try to think like your cat and search places where she may have gone. Cats like small and high spaces, so check in bushes and up in trees. Ask your neighbors and friends to help you. Do as you did in the house, using something that makes a noise your cat is familiar with. This may not work, because an indoor cat that has gotten out for the first time may be either too scared or too fascinated to pay much attention to something that the animal considers routine in her life. But it never hurts to try. Your cat may be so frightened that she *wants* you to come and rescue her.

My cat Precious has a big mouth, and if she were to get out, I know I could find her the same way I found her when she was a stray—her loud meow. She's a talker, and even being in strange places (such as the vet's office) has not stopped her from expressing herself vocally. Perhaps you know of a special quality in your own cat that may help you in finding her?

Ask your neighbors and leave your phone number with them as well as a good description of your cat so they can identify her. A good-quality photo (which you should always have in your possession) helps even more, because it gives a visual reference for folks to go by.

Get the help of police if you suspect your cat may be in a restricted area such as an abandoned building or construction site. You should never go poking around in those areas without permission or help. It could be dangerous.

Start making phone calls to area shelters, the police, veterinary hospitals, pet shops, and the like. You will want to keep in touch with any place your cat may have been taken to if she happened to have been found by someone who recognized her as a lost cat. They may have services that can help you find your cat as well. It never hurts to ask. Bring photos of your cat to these places as well and leave posters with them to either put up or hand out, or even just as a reference in case they hear or see something.

Making Posters

Place posters within a ten-mile radius of the area where your cat may have gotten lost. Place the words "LOST CAT" and "REWARD" at the top of the poster in big, dark bold letters that can be seen from the road by people driving by. Don't put on the poster the amount of the reward, however. You don't want to attract extortionists. Make sure the poster has a good picture of your cat, especially one that shows any special traits your cat may have such as an off-colored spot or an unusual marking—anything that will distinguish this cat as yours if found.

You should also place on the poster a written description of the cat. Make sure you use words that even someone who is unfamiliar with cats will understand. For example, don't put "female Cymric polydactyl," because many people do not know what a Cymric looks like or that a polydactyl is a cat with extra toes. Not everyone can tell the difference between male and female cats either, so don't bother placing the cat's gender on the poster.

Do not put your cat's name on the poster, because most cats in unfamiliar situations won't come to their name, especially if called by a stranger. Don't bother mentioning personality traits such as "will sit up and beg for food," because your cat more than likely will not be displaying her usual mannerisms. Do not mention if your cat was wearing a collar. The collar could easily have been removed or have fallen off. If you feel you must say that your cat was wearing a collar to help her be found, then word it something like this, "was wearing a red flea collar when lost, may or may not still be wearing it."

Do place your phone number as well as a backup

Start making phone calls to area shelters, the police, veterinary hospitals, pet shops, and the like—anywhere your cat may be waiting for you to come claim her.

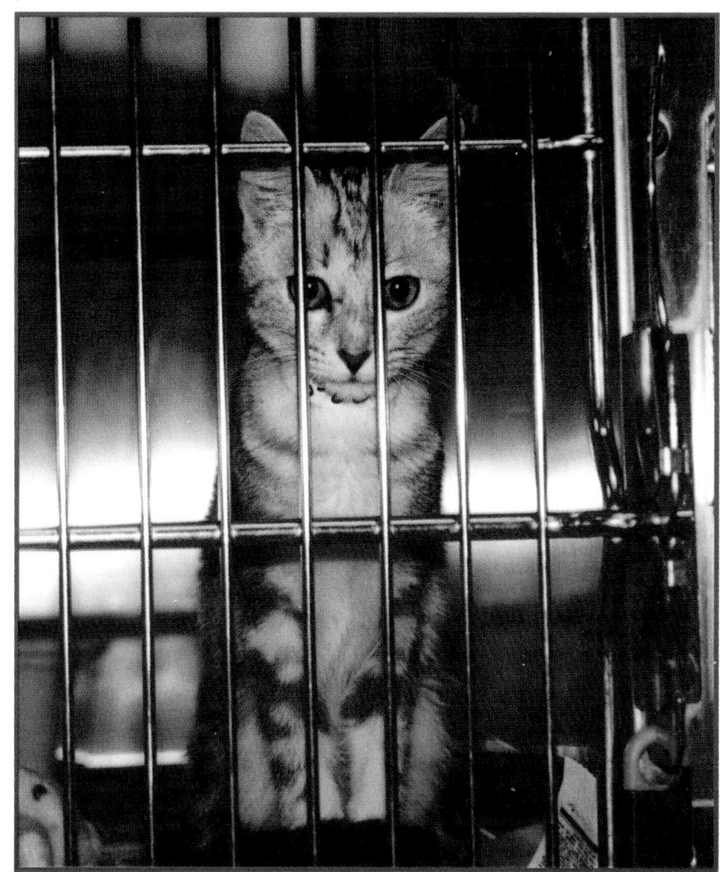

phone number on the poster, so that there is always someone available to take calls in case your kitty is found. Be sure the numbers are very visible on the poster.

Where do you place all these posters you have made? Make about 100 copies and place them everywhere; on telephone poles, signs, in store windows (with permission), at veterinary hospitals, shelters, police stations, fire stations, schools, etc. Give away copies to everyone you see, especially concentrating on the area where the cat disappeared. But keep in mind that cats can wander or even get picked up by someone and dropped off somewhere else, so widen your search to more than just the immediate area. Talk to and hand posters to mail carriers, newspaper delivery people, and anyone who runs routes where they could spot a lost animal.

Don't forget to check on your posters regularly in case they get torn off or destroyed by rain and wind. Replace them as needed.

Getting the Word Out

You can also widen your search by putting an ad in the local newspapers and checking every paper in your area as well as surrounding areas for the "Found" section, in the event someone may have picked up or seen your cat and placed an ad themselves. Some television stations have community bulletin boards where ads can be placed and lost ads can be called in and displayed on television, thus reaching more people. Radio stations may sometimes be willing to help, depending on the station (and especially if you make it sound like a real human interest story).

You can always hire a pet detective if all else fails, though this is an expensive option. But if you have the money, it may be well worth it. Believe it or not, there are very serious and very good pet detectives out there, besides Ace Ventura.

Keep Looking

Whatever you do, don't give up hope. It's very easy after a few days or a week to feel that all hope is lost and give up. But remember, some cats have been gone for weeks, months, even years, and then were found or came home on their own. Remember the book and movie, *The Incredible Journey?* Yes, it was only a story, but it was based on actual events. Cats have exceptional senses and abilities and have been known to find their way home over great distances.

When putting up posters, keep in mind that cats may wander far or even get picked up by someone and dropped off somewhere else. Widen your search if all else fails.

Whatever you do, don't give up hope that your missing cat will be found. Some cats have been gone for weeks, months, and even years before they were found or came home on their own.

Suggested Reading

TS 302
Cat Health Encyclopedia
Edited by Dr. Lowell Ackerman
320 pages, more than 200 full-color photos

TS 251
Owner's Guide to Cat Health
Dr. Lowell Ackerman
208 pages, more than 100 full-color photos

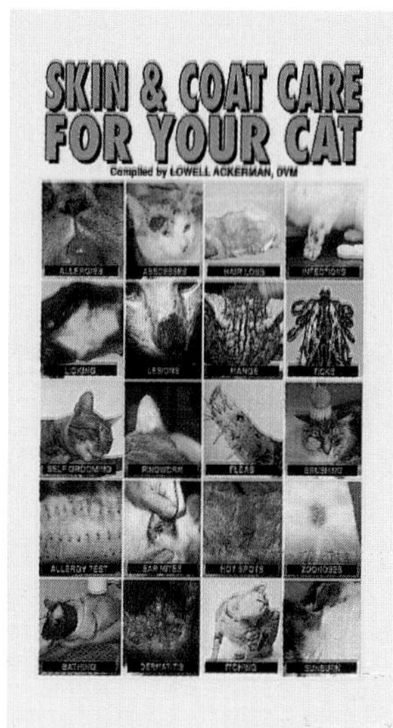

TS 250
Skin and Coat Care for Your Cat
Dr. Lowell Ackerman
160 pages, more than 100 full-color photos

TS 253
Cat Behavior and Training
Dr. Lowell Ackerman
320 pages, more than 200 full-color photos